T0390203

NEW ORLEANS SAINTS

LUKE HANLON

Apex is distributed by North Star Editions:
sales@northstareditions.com | 888-417-0195

Produced for Apex by Red Line Editorial.

Photographs ©: Kevin Terrell/AP Images, cover, 1; Michael Heiman/Getty Images Sport/Getty Images, 4–5; Gerald Herbert/AP Images, 6–7; Ferd Kaufman/AP Images, 8–9; Bettmann/Getty Images, 10–11; George Rose/Getty Images Sport/Getty Images, 12–13; Mike Powell/Allsport/Getty Images Sport/Getty Images, 14–15; Brian Bahr/Allsport/Getty Images Sport/Getty Images, 16–17; Focus On Sport/Getty Images Sport/Getty Images, 19, 22–23; James Flores/Getty Images Sport/Getty Images, 20–21; Mike Powell/Getty Images Sport/Getty Images, 24–25; Joseph Patronite/Getty Images Sport/Getty Images, 26–27; Bob Levey/WireImage/Getty Images, 28–29; Shutterstock Images, 30–31, 52–53; Elsa/Getty Images Sport/Getty Images, 32–33; Jonathan Bachman/Getty Images Sport/Getty Images, 34–35, 48–49; David Stluka/AP Images, 37, 57; Chris Graythen/Getty Images Sport/Getty Images, 38–39, 42–43; Rob Foldy/Getty Images Sport/Getty Images, 40–41; Wesley Hitt/Getty Images Sport/Getty Images, 44–45; Cooper Neill/Getty Images Sport/Getty Images, 47; Aaron M. Sprecher/AP Images, 50–51, 58–59; Kevin C. Cox/Getty Images Sport/Getty Images, 54–55

Library of Congress Control Number: 2024939371

ISBN
979-8-89250-156-9 (hardcover)
979-8-89250-173-6 (paperback)
979-8-89250-297-9 (ebook pdf)
979-8-89250-190-3 (hosted ebook)

Printed in the United States of America
Mankato, MN
012025

NOTE TO PARENTS AND EDUCATORS

Apex books are designed to build literacy skills in striving readers. Exciting, high-interest content attracts and holds readers' attention. The text is carefully leveled to allow students to achieve success quickly.

TABLE OF CONTENTS

CHAPTER 1

WHO DAT?

Fans gather outside of the Superdome. Tailgating starts early in New Orleans, Louisiana. Saints fans eat before the game. Many cook up spicy Cajun food. As kickoff nears, they fill up the dome.

Thousands of fans tailgate in the parking lot outside the Superdome before a New Orleans Saints game.

Cameron Jordan rushes the quarterback during a 2023 game against the Chicago Bears.

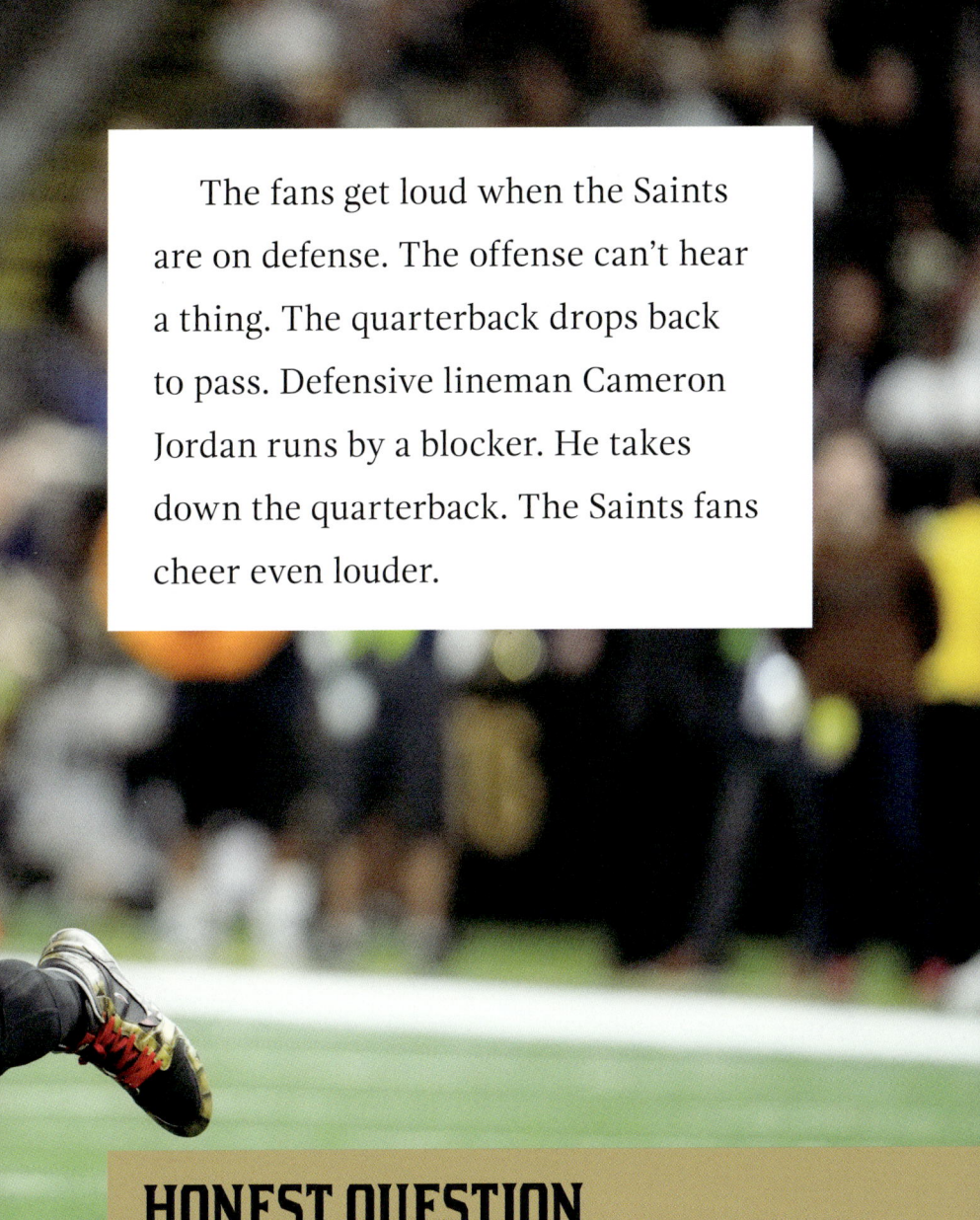

The fans get loud when the Saints are on defense. The offense can't hear a thing. The quarterback drops back to pass. Defensive lineman Cameron Jordan runs by a blocker. He takes down the quarterback. The Saints fans cheer even louder.

HONEST QUESTION

Saints fans started chanting a question in 1983. They did it before home games started. Fans yelled, "Who dat say they gonna beat dem Saints?" They have chanted it ever since.

CHAPTER 2

EARLY HISTORY

The New Orleans Saints played their first NFL season in 1967. They didn't win many games at first. But fans in New Orleans were happy to have a team. More than 80,000 people attended the Saints' first home game.

Fullback Jim Taylor (31) carries the ball during a 1967 game against the Dallas Cowboys.

Tom Dempsey kicks the game-winning 63-yard field goal in 1970.

The Saints' struggles continued for years. In 1979, they finished 8–8. That was the first time they didn't have a losing record. But the Saints couldn't keep it up. The next season, they won just one game. The team went through several coaches. But the Saints couldn't find success.

HISTORIC FIELD GOAL

In a 1970 game, the Saints were trailing 17–16. Just two seconds remained. New Orleans called on kicker Tom Dempsey. And he came through. He drilled a 63-yard field goal to win the game. At the time, it was the longest field goal in NFL history.

Jim Mora became head coach before the 1986 season. In 1987, things really turned around. Mora often gave fiery speeches. These speeches inspired the Saints. They won nine straight games. Then they made the playoffs for the first time.

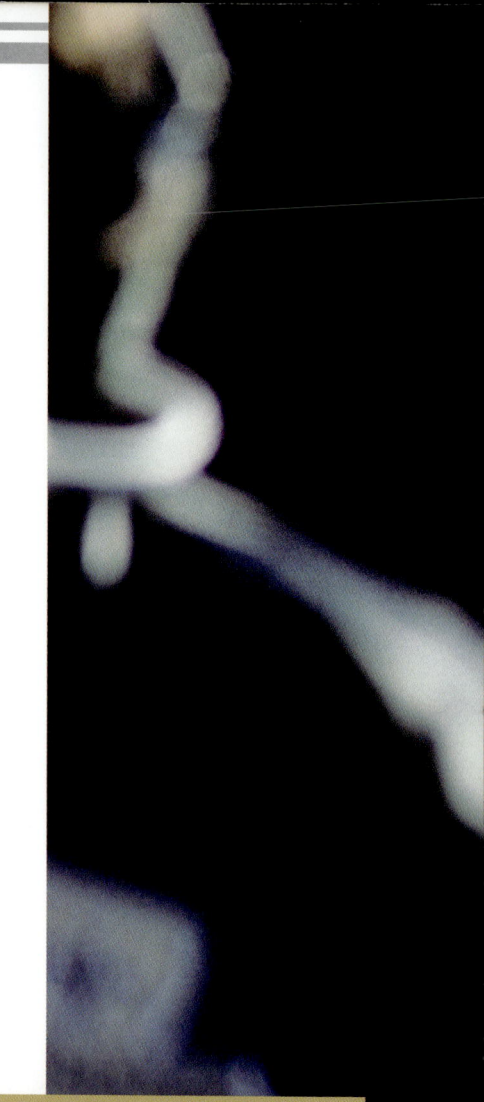

AINTS

Being a Saints fan was tough for many years. It really showed in the late 1970s. Some fans hid their faces at home games. They wore paper bags over their heads. Some bags had "Aints" written on them.

Jim Mora shouts to his players during a 1987 game.

Vaughan Johnson was a key part of the Saints' defense in the early 1990s.

The Saints lost their first playoff game. But Mora kept New Orleans competitive for years. The Saints made the playoffs in 1990, 1991, and 1992. And in 1991, they won their division for the first time. But they still couldn't win a playoff game.

STRONG DEFENSE

The Saints relied on strong defense in the early 1990s. They allowed the fewest points in the league in 1991. They did it again in 1992. New Orleans also led the NFL in sacks that season.

15

The Saints sank again after the 1992 season. They missed the playoffs the next three years. Then, in 1996, they started 0–5. Mora quit midway through the season.

The losses piled up for the rest of the 1990s. But the 2000 season brought back hope. The Saints won their division that year. Then they earned their first-ever playoff win. New Orleans beat the St. Louis Rams 31–28.

Willie Jackson scored three touchdowns during the Saints' playoff win over the St. Louis Rams.

17

RICKEY JACKSON

Rickey Jackson began his NFL career in New Orleans. The linebacker's rookie season was in 1981. He made an impact right away. He led the Saints in sacks and tackles that year. And he only got better from there.

Jackson made plays all over the field. But rushing the quarterback was his specialty. Jackson recorded at least nine sacks in eight seasons with the Saints. Many of those sacks forced fumbles. Jackson helped make the Saints' defense one of the league's best.

WHEN HE RETIRED, RICKEY JACKSON LED THE SAINTS IN CAREER SACKS, TACKLES, AND FORCED FUMBLES.

CHAPTER 3

LEGENDS

Quarterbacks didn't run much in the 1970s. But Archie Manning did. The dual-threat quarterback was a headache for defenses. Manning ran for 2,197 yards in his career. He retired in 1984. At the time, few quarterbacks had run for more yards.

Archie Manning is the father of NFL quarterbacks Peyton and Eli Manning.

The Saints' defense dominated in the late 1980s and early 1990s. A group of linebackers led the way. They earned the nickname the "Dome Patrol." Rickey Jackson and Sam Mills were two stars. Mills brought his smarts and vision to the defense. He directed others on the fly.

LEGENDARY KICKER

Few kickers have made the Pro Football Hall of Fame. But Morten Andersen did. Andersen rarely missed kicks with the Saints. He retired as the league's all-time leading scorer.

23

Pat Swilling was another member of the Dome Patrol. He found the quarterback with ease. He racked up 17 sacks in 1991. That led the NFL. Wayne Martin was another sack machine. He spent his entire 11-year career with New Orleans.

HOMETOWN HERO

Bobby Hebert was born in Louisiana. He played college football in Louisiana. And by 1987, he was the starting quarterback in New Orleans. The Saints had a winning record every year Hebert was the starter.

In 1991, Pat Swilling earned the Defensive Player of the Year Award.

Eric Martin makes a leaping catch during a playoff game in January 1993.

Eric Martin played for the Saints from 1985 to 1993. The wide receiver rarely dropped a pass. Martin recorded nearly 8,000 receiving yards with the Saints. At the time, no Saint had more.

Offensive lineman Willie Roaf protected the passer. He made his first Pro Bowl in 1994. Then he made it six more years in a row.

MEGA DEAL

The Saints really wanted Ricky Williams in 1999. They traded all their draft picks that year to get him. The running back spent only three seasons with New Orleans. But he recorded at least 1,000 total yards in two of them.

CHAPTER 4

RECENT HISTORY

Disaster struck in August 2005. Hurricane Katrina hit New Orleans. Many people died. Many more lost their homes. The Superdome was used as a shelter. The Saints played in different stadiums in 2005. They finished the season 3–13.

New Orleans residents take shelter in the Superdome after Hurricane Katrina.

In 2006, the Saints hired head coach Sean Payton. The team also returned to the Superdome. Payton led the Saints to a division title that season. Then the team reached the conference championship game. Most importantly, hope returned to the city.

HOME SWEET DOME

The Saints' first game back in the Superdome was against the Atlanta Falcons. It got off to a great start. The defense forced a punt 90 seconds into the game. Then defensive back Steve Gleason blocked the punt. The Saints recovered the ball for a touchdown. The fans erupted with joy.

In 2012, the Saints put a statue of Steve Gleason's punt block outside the Superdome.

Rebirth

25. 2006. STEVE GLEASON WAS RESPONSIBLE FOR ONE OF THE
IN NEW ORLEANS SAINTS HISTORY. HE BLOCKED A PUNT IN THE
M'S RETURN TO THE SUPERDOME FOLLOWING HURRICANE KATRINA.
ATED THEIR RIVAL ATLANTA FALCONS. 23—3. IT WOULD KICK~START
TEAM THAT WOULD GO ON TO WIN THE NFC SOUTH CROWN AND
MPIONSHIP THAT SEASON. THAT BLOCKED PUNT. THAT SEASON.
D THE "REBIRTH" OF THE CITY OF NEW ORLEANS.

The Saints made it back to the playoffs in 2009. They won two playoff games in the Superdome. These wins took them to their first Super Bowl. They faced the Indianapolis Colts. The Colts led 10–0 early. But the Saints rallied. They won 31–17.

BOLD CALL

The Saints trailed at halftime of the Super Bowl. They were kicking off to start the second half. Coach Payton knew his team needed a spark. So, he called for an onside kick. The Saints recovered. Then they scored on their next drive.

Pierre Thomas scores a leaping touchdown during the Super Bowl in early 2010.

Ted Ginn Jr. hauls in a touchdown catch during a 2017 game.

The Saints remained contenders through the 2010s. But they suffered some tough playoff losses. In 2017, the Minnesota Vikings beat them with a last-second touchdown. The next year, referees missed a penalty against the Los Angeles Rams. That led to another playoff loss. Even so, fans in New Orleans remained hopeful. They waited for another Super Bowl run.

DREW BREES

Quarterback Drew Brees entered the NFL in 2001. He spent five years with the San Diego Chargers. Then, in 2006, the Saints signed him. Brees burned through the team's record book. He set every passing record in team history.

Brees turned New Orleans into an offensive powerhouse. He led the league in passing yards seven times. He led in passing touchdowns four times. And his shining moment came in the Super Bowl against the Colts. Brees threw for 288 yards and two touchdowns. He was named Most Valuable Player (MVP) of the game.

DREW BREES THREW 491 TOUCHDOWN PASSES WITH THE SAINTS.

CHAPTER 5

MODERN STARS

Two stars led the Saints' offense in the early 2000s. Wide receiver Joe Horn provided the deep threat. Running back Deuce McAllister piled up yards on the ground. McAllister ended his career as the team leader in rushing yards.

Deuce McAllister dives over the defense for a touchdown during a 2008 game against the San Francisco 49ers.

The offense improved when Drew Brees arrived in 2006. That same year, Marques Colston broke out. The rookie quickly became Brees's go-to wide receiver. He grabbed 72 touchdown catches in New Orleans. That's more than any other Saint.

GAME OVER

Saints defensive back Tracy Porter came up big in the Super Bowl. The Colts were driving in the fourth quarter. A touchdown would have tied the game. But Porter intercepted a pass. He returned it 74 yards for a touchdown. That play sealed the win for the Saints.

Marques Colston makes a touchdown catch during a 2015 game.

Will Smith sacks the St. Louis Rams quarterback during a 2007 game.

42

Two defensive linemen led the Saints' defense. Will Smith was the first. He played from 2004 to 2012. Smith forced many fumbles. He also blocked passes. In 2011, Cameron Jordan arrived. Jordan played much like Smith. But he racked up more sacks.

RECORD BREAKER

Wide receiver Michael Thomas had a great start to his career. Then he improved in each of his next three seasons. In fact, he recorded 149 catches in 2019. That set a league record. However, injuries slowed him down after that season.

Alvin Kamara won the Offensive Rookie of the Year Award in 2017.

The team's offense added more stars in the 2010s. Tight end Jimmy Graham was a monster. He tallied 16 receiving touchdowns in 2013. That led the NFL.

Running back Mark Ingram set a new team rushing record. Then the Saints added Alvin Kamara in 2017. He became another great running back. The two had different talents. Ingram was a bruiser. Kamara was a threat in the passing game.

CAMERON JORDAN

The Saints selected Cameron Jordan with their first pick in the 2011 draft. Teams always have high hopes for first-round picks. And Jordan didn't disappoint. He quickly became the heart of the Saints' defense.

The defensive lineman did it all. He stopped the run. He was also great at rushing the passer. Jordan's best skill was his consistency. Season after season, he played at a high level. Jordan recorded at least 7.5 sacks 11 seasons in a row. Only two other NFL players have ever done that.

IN 2022, CAMERON JORDAN MADE HIS EIGHTH PRO BOWL WITH NEW ORLEANS.

CHAPTER 6

TEAM TRIVIA

New Orleans is known for jazz music. In fact, jazz inspired the Saints' name. It comes from "When the Saints Go Marching In." That's one of the most famous jazz songs.

The Preservation Hall Jazz Band is one of the best-known jazz groups in New Orleans.

The Saints played their first eight seasons in a college stadium. Then in 1975, the Superdome opened. The Saints have played there ever since. The Superdome is one of the oldest stadiums in the NFL. But it has been updated several times.

The Superdome can hold more than 70,000 fans.

SUPER HOST

The Superdome has an apt name. No stadium has hosted the Super Bowl more times. The Superdome was chosen to host the big game in the 2024 season. That was the eighth time the Superdome had been chosen to host the game.

Mercedes-Benz Superdome

The United States bought Louisiana from France in 1803. The Saints decided to honor the state's French history. The team's logo is an old French symbol. The symbol is called the fleur-de-lis. In English, that means "lily flower." The team began using the logo in 1967.

TIMELESS JERSEYS

As with their logo, the Saints haven't changed their jerseys much. Their three main colors are black, gold, and white. Every jersey since 1967 has featured at least two of those three colors.

The fleur-de-lis appears on the Saints' helmets.

In 2022, Payton Turner (98) blocked a field goal to beat the Atlanta Falcons.

The Saints' biggest rival is the Atlanta Falcons. The teams first played each other in 1967. In 1970, they became part of the same division. So, they play twice a year. Going into 2024, the Saints had the most regular-season wins.

THE PUNT BLOCKER RETURNS

Steve Gleason made a huge punt block in 2006. That game was against the Falcons. Nine years later, Gleason attended a Saints home game against the Falcons. He was there just as a fan. But once again, the Saints blocked a punt for a touchdown.

TEAM RECORDS

All-Time Passing Yards: 68,010
Drew Brees (2006–20)

All-Time Touchdown Passes: 491
Drew Brees (2006–20)

All-Time Rushing Yards: 6,500
Mark Ingram (2011–18, 2021–22)

All-Time Rushing Touchdowns: 54
Alvin Kamara (2017–)

All-Time Receiving Yards: 9,759
Marques Colston (2006–15)

All-Time Interceptions: 37
Dave Waymer (1980–89)

All-Time Sacks: 123*
Rickey Jackson (1981–93)

All-Time Scoring: 1,318
Morten Andersen (1982–94)

All-Time Coaching Wins: 152
Sean Payton (2006–11, 2013–21)

Super Bowl Titles: 1
(2009)

Sacks were not an official statistic until 1982. However, researchers have studied old games to determine sacks dating back to 1960.

All statistics are accurate through 2023.

TIMELINE

1967 — 1975 — 1987 — 1991 — 2000

The New Orleans Saints play their first NFL season.

The Saints make the playoffs for the first time.

The Saints win their first playoff game.

The Saints play their first game at the Superdome.

The Saints win their division for the first time.

2005 **2006** **2009** **2018** **2022**

After signing Drew Brees and hiring Sean Payton, the Saints make a run to the conference championship game.

The Saints play in their first conference championship game since 2009.

Hurricane Katrina hits New Orleans, forcing the Saints to play in other cities all season.

The Saints make their first Super Bowl and beat the Indianapolis Colts.

Dennis Allen replaces Sean Payton as the team's head coach.

COMPREHENSION QUESTIONS

Write your answers on a separate piece of paper.

1. Write a paragraph that explains the main ideas of Chapter 2.

2. Who do you think was the greatest player in New Orleans Saints history? Why?

3. In the 2009 season, which team did the Saints beat in the Super Bowl?
   A. Indianapolis Colts
   B. Minnesota Vikings
   C. Seattle Seahawks

4. Why would a dual-threat quarterback create problems for defenders?
   A. Defenders have to focus on both long and short passes.
   B. Defenders have to focus on onside kicks.
   C. Defenders have to focus on both the pass and the run.

5. What does **consistency** mean in this book?

*Jordan's best skill was his **consistency**. Season after season, he played at a high level.*

    A. good at only one thing

    B. slower than most other players

    C. able to stay the same over time

6. What does **apt** mean in this book?

*The Superdome has an **apt** name. No stadium has hosted the Super Bowl more times.*

    A. fitting

    B. out of place

    C. common

Answer key on page 64.

GLOSSARY

Cajun food
A spicy style of cooking from Louisiana that mixes French, Spanish, and West African elements.

conference
A group of teams that make up part of a sports league.

deep threat
A wide receiver who catches deep passes.

division
In the NFL, a group of teams that make up part of a conference.

draft
A system that lets teams select new players coming into the league.

dual-threat
Able to throw and run as a quarterback.

fumbles
When players lose control of the ball.

intercepted
Caught an opponent's pass as a defensive player.

onside kick
A short kickoff that the kicking team tries to recover.

playoffs
A set of games played after the regular season to decide which team is the champion.

sacks
Plays that happen when a defender tackles the quarterback before he can throw the ball.

TO LEARN MORE

BOOKS

Anderson, Josh. *New Orleans Saints*. Mankato,
  MN: The Child's World, 2022.
Coleman, Ted. *New Orleans Saints All-Time
  Greats*. Mendota Heights, MN: Press Box Books,
  2022.
Mattern, Joanne. *New Orleans Saints*.
  Minneapolis: Bellwether Media, 2023.

ONLINE RESOURCES

Visit **www.apexeditions.com** to find links and
resources related to this title.

ABOUT THE AUTHOR

Luke Hanlon is a sportswriter, editor, and author
based in Minneapolis. He watches NFL games all day
on Sundays during the fall.

INDEX

ANSWER KEY:

1. Answers will vary; 2. Answers will vary; 3. A; 4. C; 5. C; 6.